# Contents

# Let's Discuss

# DRINKING

## Ronda Armitage

Wayland

# Let's Discuss

The case studies in this
book are fictitious. They ar
subject to copyright and m
reproduced for use in the c

First published in 1987 by
Wayland (Publishers) Limit
61 Western Road, Hove
East Sussex BN3 1JD, Engla

**British Library Cataloguing
Publication Data**
Armitage, Ronda
  Drinking.
  1. Alcoholism 2. Alcohol—
  logical effect
  I Title
  613.8'1   RC565

ISBN 0–85078–913–3

Typeset, printed and bound
in the UK at
The Bath Press, Avon

# Introduction

Alcohol is a substance which when it is used wisely can give pleasure and benefit to many people, but it is also a drug which can cause enormous misery and damage and can destroy life.

The aim of this book is to give some information to people who will soon be beginning to drink, in order that they may enjoy their drinking and not be harmed by it. For many young people alcohol can seem rather like a 'magic key'; it can appear to open the doors to popularity, 'love' and social success. Although it can be useful in social situations, it can also all too easily become a crutch that people lean on.

As far as possible this book tries to avoid the word 'alcoholic'. This is because certain myths seem to have grown up around the word. Firstly there is the idea that only certain people become alcoholics, that alcoholics are born, not made. There is no evidence to support this. Anybody, of whatever age, if they drink often enough and excessively enough may develop alcohol problems. They may even become dependent on alcohol. The second myth is that you are an alcoholic only if you drink in certain ways: for example if you drink on your own and hide alcohol away to conceal the habit. This may well be true for some people who are alcohol-dependent—there is often much guilt and shame felt by the person who is drinking—but for others alcoholism may simply be social drinking that has got out of hand.

*Many people tend to associate the word 'alcoholic' with down-and-outs, yet everyone who drinks can become addicted to alcohol.*

# What Is Alcohol?

Ethyl alcohol, or ethanol, is a clear, colourless liquid made up of the chemical elements carbon, hydrogen and oxygen. Its chemical formula is $C_2H_5OH$. Although there are other alcohols used for other purposes, ethyl alcohol is the only alcohol that can be drunk. For the rest of this book ethyl alcohol will be referred to as alcohol.

Although alcohol can be made artificially by chemists in a laboratory, it is more usually prepared through a natural process called fermentation. Fermentation occurs when yeast fungi ferment certain sugars in fruits and plants to form carbon dioxide and alcohol. Wine is made in this way from grapes, cider from apples and beer from barley. Fermentation gives quite a weak solution of alcohol. Spirits such as gin, whisky and vodka, which have a greater concentration of alcohol, are produced by a process called distillation.

*Yeast is added to a mixture of malt, water and sugar to ferment it into beer in a large commercial brewery.*

*Workers shovelling grapes into a wine press in France. The grapes are crushed in the press to provide the juice which is eventually fermented to produce wine.*

In Britain there are three main kinds of alcoholic drinks: beers, wines and spirits. Beer is still the biggest-selling form of alcohol in Britain. It is made by mixing malt, which is barley grains that have been allowed to germinate, with hot water. Sugar, yeast and hops are also added. Much of the beer drunk in Britain is produced here, although a small amount comes in from Europe, the USA and even Australia.

Most of the wine drunk in Britain is imported from Europe, with France, Italy, West Germany and Spain being the main exporters. Some wine also comes from California, South America and Australia. A very small amount is produced in the south of England.

Most wine is made from grapes. Yeast occurs naturally on ripe grapes as the thin, waxy coating called 'the bloom'. When the yeast reacts with the sugar in the grapes, fermentation occurs. Red wine is made from red grapes, but white wine may be made from either white grapes or red grapes without their skins. Fortified wines, such as sherry and port, are produced by adding a spirit, usually brandy, to a wine base.

The spirits most often drunk in Britain are gin, whisky, brandy, vodka and rum. They are produced by distillation, which is the process of boiling and separating the more volatile alcohol from the other fluids. It is a more complicated process than fermentation and many spirits have to age for several years before they are ready to be drunk. This is one of the reasons why a bottle of whisky costs considerably more than a bottle of table wine.

Cider is another drink that needs to be mentioned because many people think of it as traditionally English. It is produced from fermented apple juice. Although it has grown in popularity over the last few years it still occupies a fairly small proportion of the drinks market.

Beers and wines are allowed to be sold in this country without any indication on the cans or bottles of the percentage of alcohol they contain. Generally speaking, the average strength of beer is 3.7 per cent alcohol by volume. Some export lagers may be rather stronger, with as much as 8 per cent alcohol by volume. Percentage by volume figures show us what percentage of a given drink is alcohol; what is not alcohol is mostly water.

Cider has roughly the same alcohol content as beer. Like beer, however, it varies. Some strong ciders may be as much as 13.5 per cent alcohol. There is very little variation in the strength of wines: almost all table wines

*A Scottish whisky distillery. The distillation process needs to be closely controlled if the end product is going to come up to standard.*

contain 11 per cent alcohol. The strength of spirits is fixed by law and is indicated by the 'proof' level shown on the label of the bottles. The proof system is rather complicated and is gradually being replaced by the percentage by volume system in Britain. Whisky, gin and brandy all contain 40 per cent alcohol; vodka contains 37 per cent alcohol. Obviously a pint of undiluted spirits will be more powerful than a pint of beer, so spirits are usually diluted by adding mixers such as water, lemonade or tonic.

*This diagram shows the alcohol content of some of the most commonly consumed alcoholic drinks.*

1 *Having read the percentage by volume figures for various alcoholic drinks, would you think that drinking beer would have fairly little effect on you?*

2 *Do you think that different drinks have different 'images'? For instance, if you saw one person drinking a glass of wine and another person drinking a measure of whisky, who would you think was the heavier drinker?*

3 *Should all alcoholic drinks have to show percentage by volume figures on their labels?*

# The Origins of Alcohol

The very first alcoholic drink was probably discovered by accident. Fermentation can occur in any of a number of sugar-containing substances, such as grapes, berries or honey, if they are left exposed in warm conditions. One Persian legend tells of a king who loved grapes and who stored ripe grapes in a cellar so that he would have a year-long supply. Some bruised grapes began to ferment, thus giving off carbon dioxide gas which knocked out some of the slaves who worked in the cellar. One of the king's unwanted mistresses, thinking to poison herself with this potion, disappeared into the cellar. She emerged some time later singing and dancing and in high spirits. The Persian king was not slow to realize how useful this concoction might be for keeping his subjects happy.

There is enough evidence available to support the belief that the making of beer and wine has been going on since at least 5000BC. From its earliest days, the making and drinking of alcohol assumed an important role in all sorts of personal, social and religious occasions. It was, and still is, drunk at births, deaths, initiations, marriages, crownings and feasts of all kinds.

*A historical illustration of Scottish New Year celebrations.*

It was offered in hospitality and sometimes even reputed to have magical powers. It assisted the warrior in feeling more aggressive in war and helped to relax him when the time came for peacemaking.

Early civilizations also discovered the less beneficial aspects of drinking alcohol. In the Egyptian and Mesopotamian civilizations, drunkenness was quite a problem. It was recognized that the result of excessive drinking was often acute, and sometimes chronic, illness. The government in Babylonia in 1770BC was so concerned that it introduced what were probably the first licensing laws. These laws operated in much the same way as those of today, controlling the times and places at which alcoholic drinks could be sold.

Phoenician traders and the Romans were probably the first peoples to introduce the Ancient Britons to the process of making alcohol, but more certain evidence of brewing in England came with the growth and spread of Christianity. Not only did Christian monks brew much of the country's beer, but it would seem they also drank it in large quantities. Gildas, a monk living in the fifth century AD, admonished his brother monks thus: 'If any monk through drinking too freely gets thick of speech so that he cannot join the psalmody, he is to be deprived of his supper.'

The brewing of ale was a major cottage industry by AD1100. It was brewed mostly by women known as alewives. Because of the lack of sanitation in those days, it was often safer to drink a weak ale than to drink water. As

*In the early days of brewing, monasteries were major centres for the making, and drinking, of beer.*

*A medieval merchant pays 'wine tax' to the clergy. People in power have long seen alcohol as a means of raising money.*

a result, it was customary to give it to children of all ages. The twelfth century also saw the first levying of a national tax on ale. Henry II raised the money to pay for the war against Saladin, the sultan of Egypt and Syria. The taxation of fermented beverages has continued uninterrupted ever since.

By the 1500s whisky and other distilled spirits were in evidence in Britain. Many whisky distilleries on the west coast of Scotland were sited where early monasteries had existed. The popularity of whisky spread, no doubt aided by its reputation as a medicine which had beneficial effects on health. It was also said to prolong life and cure a wide range of illnesses, including smallpox.

The eighteenth century saw the beginnings of the rise of the modern temperance movement, mainly in the United States but also in Britain. People who joined the movement were concerned about the rights and wrongs of drinking alcohol and the effect alcohol had on the way people behaved. The movement became stronger throughout the nineteenth century and in

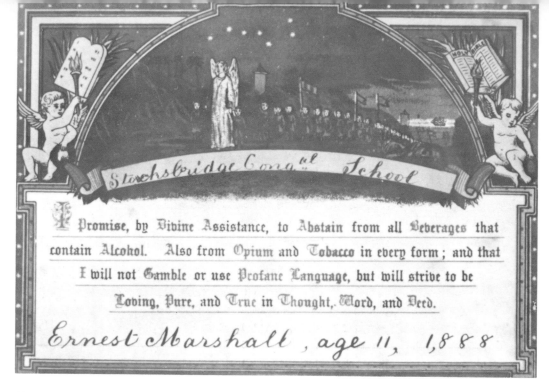

*A nineteenth-century temperance pledge card.*

1919 prohibition laws were passed in the United States which made the making and selling of alcohol illegal. These laws were repealed in 1933.

Our modern licensing laws were introduced during the First World War (1914–18) by Lloyd George. It had been suggested after the Battle of Neuve Chapelle in France that one of the reasons for the British failure was lack of shells. The munitions workers were blamed. They were alleged to make a lot of money and to pass their days drinking in public houses. Legislation was brought in to restrict the hours when pubs were open and to impose a gap in the afternoon when drinkers must be turned out.

---

1  *Do you think prohibition could ever be introduced, and succeed, in Britain?*
2  *If alcohol sales were not so profitable for governments in the form of taxes, would more be done to limit drinking?*

*'Britain's out-dated licensing laws are bound up with the country's class structure. They were introduced to make sure the working classes worked, and this distrust of the people by the authorities still exists today. The government is thinking of changing the laws because foreign tourists find them inconvenient, not because it trusts the population to behave responsibly.' Discuss.*

---

# The Effects of Alcohol

Many people take alcoholic drinks without really understanding what alcohol is or what it does to them. They think of alcohol as a pleasant way of adding to the enjoyment of social activities. They may feel more relaxed after a few drinks or perhaps more confident and better prepared to join in a social occasion. What many people do not realize, however, is that alcohol is a depressant drug.

Some drugs act as a 'pep up', making people feel more lively and better able to cope. These drugs are called stimulants. Drugs which are used to calm people and to lessen their anxieties are called depressants. They depress the nervous system. The drug alcohol is rather deceptive in its effects. Because a few drinks seem to act as a stimulant by making the drinker feel better and perhaps more buoyant, many people find it difficult to accept what is actually happening. Alcohol is like an anaesthetic: it progressively puts the brain to sleep glass by glass. It lessens the brain's power

*Although many people use alcohol to make them feel sociable, the drug can have a depressant effect.*

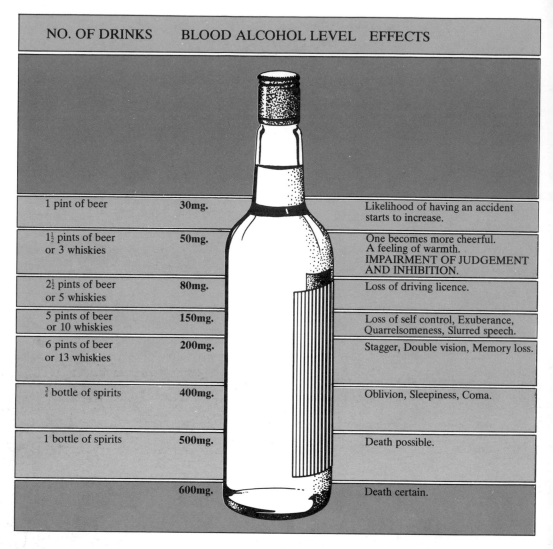

| NO. OF DRINKS | BLOOD ALCOHOL LEVEL | EFFECTS |
|---|---|---|
| 1 pint of beer | 30mg. | Likelihood of having an accident starts to increase. |
| 1½ pints of beer or 3 whiskies | 50mg. | One becomes more cheerful. A feeling of warmth. IMPAIRMENT OF JUDGEMENT AND INHIBITION. |
| 2½ pints of beer or 5 whiskies | 80mg. | Loss of driving licence. |
| 5 pints of beer or 10 whiskies | 150mg. | Loss of self control, Exuberance, Quarrelsomeness, Slurred speech. |
| 6 pints of beer or 13 whiskies | 200mg. | Stagger, Double vision, Memory loss. |
| ¾ bottle of spirits | 400mg. | Oblivion, Sleepiness, Coma. |
| 1 bottle of spirits | 500mg. | Death possible. |
| | 600mg. | Death certain. |

*A diagram showing the effects of alcohol on the average drinker.*

to make judgements and adversely affects self-control and skills, so that after a few drinks people are no longer making considered decisions. You may have heard the expression 'it is the drink talking', and while this is only a figurative description, alcohol does have a considerable effect on what a drinker is saying or doing.

Once alcohol has been drunk, it takes some time before it is eliminated from the body. Some alcohol is absorbed within a few minutes, but the rest passes into the blood via the small intestine. The blood circulates to the heart and is then pumped to other parts of the body including the brain. Only when it passes through the liver is it cleansed of alcohol. It will take the body about three hours to get rid of two units of alcohol, that is to say one pint of beer or two glasses of wine.

It is possible to gauge the amount of alcohol in the blood. This is done by checking how much alcohol (which is always measured in milligrams) is present per 100 millilitres of blood. After a 70-kg man has drunk one pint of beer, the level of alcohol in the blood will have risen to about 30 mg per 100 ml.

The exact amount of alcohol that is absorbed into the blood stream will depend on how much alcohol has been drunk, how quickly it has been drunk, whether the person had eaten before drinking and the weight of the person concerned. Women are usually affected more quickly by alcohol than are men. This is partially due to the fact that they are generally smaller and lighter.

If alcohol is used unwisely or excessively it can damage many parts of the body. It can also cause alcohol addiction, but that will be discussed in a later chapter. It affects the brain by destroying brain cells; this in turn can lead to brain damage. Loss of memory and weakened control of judgement and physical movement are common results of brain damage. Too much drinking also causes the liver to become fatty, scarred and diseased. This condition is called cirrhosis and causes a considerable number of deaths each year. Women are more vulnerable to this disease than men.

*Alcohol can influence behaviour in a variety of ways; aggression and violence are two of its less acceptable results.*

*Drinking affects most workers' performance, but for people such as firemen it can make the difference between life and death.*

Alcohol inflames the lining of the mouth, the throat and the stomach. Apart from causing vomiting if taken in excess, it also increases the risk of duodenal ulcers and is associated with both mouth and throat cancers. Alcohol's very high calorie count means that not only do heavy drinkers tend to put on weight, but the alcohol also causes the heart to become fatty. This increases the risk of heart failure.

As well as these gradual effects on a drinker's health, alcohol can cause damage and even death soon after being drunk. A single large intake of alcohol can kill by stopping the breathing. It is therefore wise to check people who are 'sleeping it off', as they may actually have lost consciousness and be in need of urgent medical attention.

The exact effect that alcohol will have on a person's behaviour is hard to predict. It depends on the amount drunk, the personality and the age of the individual and his or her mood at the time of drinking. Predictable or not, alcohol does affect behaviour to a greater or lesser degree. Some people will take greater risks than normal, some may become boisterous or aggressive, while others may become depressed or perhaps simply go to sleep.

It may take a large number of drinks before older people start behaving aggressively or foolishly, but in the young far fewer drinks are needed. Some girls may find themselves in sexual trouble while male youths are more likely to become involved in fights. For youngsters of both sexes, the risks that they take on the roads after drinking can often end in serious accidents or even in death.

Drinking has been recognized by experts as a contributing factor in many criminal activities. A recent British study found that of 400 male prisoners, excluding short-term drunkenness offenders, over half had a serious drinking problem. Many of the prisoners stated that they had committed crimes, particularly burglaries, after drinking.

Drinking has also been established as a possible cause of many accidents, and not just those that occur on the roads. Although no hard evidence is available for accidents at homes or in factories, one study of 300 consecutive deaths from unintentional injuries found that 30 per cent of those who died were known to be heavy drinkers or alcoholics.

People whose health and alertness of mind are vital to their careers will tend to steer clear of alcohol, because of its effects. Sportsmen and sports-women, for instance, find that the physical and psychological changes brought about by alcohol (except in small amounts) can be detrimental to their performance. Similarly, members of the fire service, the medical profession and any people working with machinery are well aware of the dangers of alcohol, as it can affect their alertness for some time after being drunk.

½ pint of beer   1 glass of table wine   1 glass of sherry   1 single whisky   1 unit of alcohol

# Case Study 1:

## Sarah, aged 26

It is four years now since Sarah started running marathons. 'I really started by accident,' she explains. 'One evening I had joined my husband when he went on his rugby training run. He was quite impressed and suggested that I train more seriously, so I did. Now I train twice a day and in between I look after my husband and our two children and also do a part-time job.'

Sarah's lifestyle leaves her very little time for socializing and drinking, but this does not concern her greatly. 'Before I started running seriously,' she says, 'I would go out more, which gave me more opportunities for drinking than I have now. It was not that I needed alcohol more in the past, just that I found myself more often in situations where alcohol was available and where you were expected to drink it. If you didn't, people would wonder what was wrong with you.'

Now she has taken up marathon-running, Sarah makes fairly strict rules for herself where alcohol is concerned: 'I don't touch it for three weeks before a big run, although I know some runners who leave themselves only a week. Sometimes I may be tempted to have just a glass of sherry or wine, but never within three days of a race. Alcohol is very dehydrating and when you are doing a marathon, you need to conserve as much moisture as possible.

'There are also other dangers for runners, particularly with beers and lagers. If these are drunk before someone undergoes physical exercise, the gassiness can cause stomach cramps. They are very painful—I know because I have had them.

'What I have to do before a race is eliminate anything at all that may cause a bad performance. Neither drink nor cigarettes will help me to give my best, so I don't touch them. People always ask me if running is worthwhile when I have to sacrifice "so many other things", but that is not the way I look at it. Alcohol does not often make me feel any better and too much alcohol always makes me feel worse, so I do not feel that I am missing out on anything.'

Opposite: *Alcohol can cause great physical damage if taken in excess, but even in moderation it causes dehydration. As a result, athletes in general, and long-distance runners in particular, tend to avoid it near the times when they are competing.*

1   Do you think it is sufficiently understood that alcohol is a drug?
2   Do some of the facts in the preceding chapter surprise you? Do you think there is enough information available on the effects of drinking?
3   Does the idea of being 'out of control' after drinking excite or frighten you?

'Our understanding of the effects of alcohol is seriously impaired by the common notions that drinking is sociable and drunkenness is funny. Unless we can counteract these ideas, there will be no real decline in alcohol-related deaths.' Debate whether this is a fair comment.

# Advertising Alcohol

There are many different reasons why people drink, but one of the most widely accepted reasons is that we do it so that we will be rather different people. Not only will we feel differently ourselves after a drink, but somehow we will be seen differently by others. We will be more confident, more witty and more amusing. We will perhaps feel more powerful and more attractive to the opposite sex.

These myths about alcohol have grown up over hundreds of years and are deeply ingrained in our culture and its customs. Advertisers do not invent the myths, but they do use them to sell alcohol. There is obviously not a single drink advertisement which suggests that people will become boastful, silly and possibly angry after drinking. Instead advertisements tend to emphasize either the companionable or the more glamorous aspects of sipping a particular drink. In a typical advertisement handsome men and beautiful, fashionable women gaze into each other's eyes on some exotic island and sip an 'exciting' aperitif. The idea of the advertisement is of course to persuade us that if we want to appear beautiful and wordly-wise, perhaps we too should drink this particular product.

*The image of sophistication that many advertisers seek to associate with alcoholic products has little relevance to the reality of drinking, yet its continued use bears witness to its success.*

*More women than ever before now drink in pubs and advertising agencies have been quick to exploit this development.*

Advertising probably does not create a social trend, although there seems to be little doubt that it reflects and reinforces it. An example of this can be seen in the changing patterns of women's drinking since the Second World War. For various social reasons, considerably more women are now drinking both at home and in public places than were forty years ago. The image of the drinking woman is acceptable today in a way which would have been impossible just after the war. The advertising of alcohol did not make this happen, but the drinks companies were quick to notice that it was happening and to encourage it. Advertisements for alcoholic drinks have greatly increased in number over the years, and nowhere more so than in women's magazines.

All this would seem to suggest that the drinks industry can advertise where and how it likes without due regard to any of the problems or dangers associated with alcohol. In fact in Britain and in some other countries there is a code of advertising practice which has been agreed by the manufacturers of alcoholic drinks with the Advertising Standards Authority. The code is designed to protect young people and other vulnerable groups from being unduly influenced by advertising.

Under the terms of this code, British advertisements for alcoholic drinks should not be directed at young people, nor should they in any way encourage them to start drinking. Anyone shown drinking must be obviously older than 18 and children should not be depicted in advertisements except where it would be usual for them to appear, such as in family scenes or in background crowds. They should never be shown drinking alcoholic beverages nor should it be implied that they are.

Besides those relating to minors, there are also a number of other rules governing the advertising of alcohol. People cannot be shown to have failed if they do not accept the challenge of a particular drink and no adverts are allowed which emphasize the stimulant, sedative or tranquillizing effects of any drink.

It is, however, quite legitimate for a drinks company to advertise its products by indicating that they give pleasure to many, are of high quality and are widely enjoyed in all classes of society. It may also seek to persuade people to change brands and can provide information on new products. In pursuit of these objectives, advertisers may employ such techniques of presentation, including humour, fantasy, symbolism and allusion, as are used by the advertisers of other categories of product or service.

*Does the humour of many advertisements for drinks blind the public to the very real dangers of alcohol?*

*Advertising outside an off-licence in London. Critics believe that the great numbers of drinks advertisements cause people to see alcohol as a part of everyday life, rather than something they can choose to drink or not to drink.*

From time to time the morality of advertising alcohol has been questioned. At the 1985 British Medical Association's annual conference, for instance, it was suggested that the advertising of alcohol products should be banned. It was recognized some years ago that cigarette smoking is harmful to people's health and as a result cigarette advertising has been banned on television. Alcohol, however, which is a drug which can cause chronic illness and death in those who misuse it, has as yet suffered no major restrictions as regards its advertising. Perhaps the fact that tax revenue from alcohol earns the Treasury well over £2,000 million each year could account for the reluctance of successive governments to curtail the advertising of this product.

# Case Study 2:

## Adrian, aged 31

Adrian is an account executive with an advertising agency which does quite a lot of work for the drinks industry. Adrian explains how his agency would go about advertising an alcoholic product on behalf of the manufacturer: 'Let's imagine in this case that the client is a drinks company with a new product called Pow. The company will already have a certain amount of information: their market research team, for instance, will have discovered whom the target audience is, that is those people who are most likely to buy the drink. In this case, let us say that the company has found that Pow will appeal most to the under-30s.

'The target audience determines the style and design of the advertising campaign, which is likely to cover cinemas, magazines, newspapers and billboards, as well as television. Obviously the moving ads, that is television and cinema commercials, give our creative team the most scope for coming up with a scenario. As Pow is meant to sell to the younger set, the team will probably put forward a scenario that is fast-moving, jumping from scene to scene, and that suggests Pow is a "fun" drink. This would mean that the background could well be something like a holiday scene.'

Adrian admits that the advertising of alcoholic drinks is seldom realistic, often relying on humour to cover over the one-sidedness of its presentation. 'But of course,' he says, 'we have to try to emphasize the better points of what we are selling. After all, we are not likely to have a satisfied client if we show someone who is obviously drunk lying on a park bench, trying to keep himself warm with newspaper and clutching a bottle of Pow.'

The power of drinks advertising has never been greater, Adrian believes, and he puts this down to the fact that alcohol has now become subject to fashion and people are more willing than ever to try something different. On the morality of advertising alcohol, Adrian has very firm views: 'It is not, as far as I am concerned, a moral question. We simply promote a drink, we do not promote drunkenness—the two things are completely separate. It is exactly the same as sports car advertising: it is the car that is being promoted, not the reckless driving that some people might use it for. It is in this light that any discussion of alcohol advertising must be conducted.'

*Most advertisers seek to give their products a glamorous image, but is this especially wrong in the case of alcohol?*

1 Do you agree with Adrian that there are no moral questions raised by the advertising of alcohol?
2 Advertisers of alcohol are allowed to use the same 'techniques of presentation' as advertisers of other products. Is this reasonable or should alcohol be a specially restricted case?
3 Do you think your view of drinking is influenced by what you see in advertisements?
4 Can you think of any practical ways of making alcohol advertisements give a more accurate picture? Would it be a good idea, for instance, if all the advertisements had to carry a health warning, in the way that cigarette advertisements do?

# Drinking at the Pub

The pub, or public house, is a British institution which does not exist in the same form anywhere else in the world. There are other public places, such as wine bars and restaurants, where alcohol is allowed to be sold and drunk, but the British generally still prefer to do their drinking at the local pub.

*Pubs have been in existence for centuries. In the past, however, they were usually very simply furnished and offered only a very limited selection of food and drink.*

*Many young people grow up with the idea that social events must involve the drinking of alcohol. As a result, pubs and clubs are becoming increasingly important in their social lives.*

In many areas the pub is more than just a drinking place; it is often the focal point of the community, a centre where local events and meetings can take place. It is also increasingly a place where young people come together, particularly in country areas where perhaps there are few public facilities for them. This is of concern to many publicans. On the one hand they recognize the need for young people to have a meeting place, and indeed many would say that youngsters are safer in a pub than wandering the streets. On the other hand, however, it is the responsibility of publicans to help enforce the law. The law states that with one exception it is illegal to sell alcohol to people under the age of 18. If the publican is discovered not carrying out the requirements of the law, then he or she faces the possibility of losing their licence and therefore their livelihood.

The law relating to minors, pubs and the sale of alcohol is very complicated. It is perfectly legal for children to be on pub premises if special facilities such as a children's room or a restaurant are provided. Young people of 14 and over may enter the bar, but they can only buy non-alcoholic drinks and should be accompanied by an adult. Youngsters between the ages of 16 and 18 who are eating a meal in a dining room or a room set aside for seated meals may buy and drink perry, cider and beer. They may not buy spirits or wine. This is the only exception to the law forbidding the sale of alcoholic drinks to people under 18, whether it be at licensed premises or at other outlets such as supermarkets.

Young people, whether entitled or not, enter a pub and drink at the publican's discretion. Publicans have the same rights under the Sale of Goods Act as, say, shopkeepers. They are not obliged to sell anything to anyone if they do not want to. They are also entitled to call for police help if someone refuses to leave the premises or if any trouble occurs.

*Pubs have traditionally been seen as places where people, and men in particular, can meet and talk. They are changing, however, in response to new drinking patterns.*

*A growing number of pubs now serve meals and a wider selection of non-alcoholic drinks.*

It is interesting to note that not only does the pub act as a local meeting place in real life but also in fiction. In many of Britain's 'soap operas', much of the action takes place in the local pub, whether it be the Queen Vic, the Rover's Return or the Bull. As far as programme producers are concerned, the pub is a useful device, because it provides a place where all members of the fictional cast may conveniently come together. Some parents and teachers, however, have expressed concern at how the pub seems to predominate in so much of young people's television viewing. They feel that youths may come to equate adulthood with being able to drink rather than with other equally pleasurable and possibly less harmful occupations.

Pubs, however, are changing. More and more of them now offer a much wider range of both drinks and food. Coffee, fruit juices and non-alcoholic beers and wines are more easily obtained than in the past. Many pubs have also converted parts of their premises into restaurants where sit-down meals are available. These changes may mean the pub can in the future become a meeting place not only for those who drink alcohol but also for those who choose not to.

# Case Study 3:

# Margaret, aged 49

Margaret has been the tenant of a small village pub since the early 1970s. She had been working in the pub for some time before being given the tenancy by the brewery. 'In those days,' she says, 'running a pub was considered a man's job and so quite a few people were surprised when I took over.'

As Margaret's pub is owned by the brewery, she has to open it up every day of the year except Christmas Day. 'I open the doors at 10.30 am each morning,' she says, 'but really that is a bit early for our village. It's most unusual to have anyone in before 11.30. I wish publicans had more of a say in their opening hours, as they do in many parts of Europe. Sometimes of an evening when we've got a good crowd in, it would be fun if we could stay open after 10.30 pm. But the law is the law, so I call last orders at 10.20 and everyone must have left the premises by 10.45.'

Margaret has found that her trade has changed a good deal over the years she has been at the pub. When she first started as a barmaid, the pub was basically just somewhere to drink beer and to have a chat. Now other drinks and food are becoming increasingly important. Margaret has mixed feelings about this: 'I feel obliged to provide food, because if I don't I will lose customers, but I do find it something of a nuisance. It has also required a lot of expensive equipment, like the new microwave.'

When asked about her customers, Margaret replies: 'They are quite a mixed bunch really. In the early evening we have a group of commuters who drop in for an hour or so before they go home, then later on people from the farming community will call in after their evening meal for a pint, a chat and maybe a game of darts or pool. We have two pool tables and two dartboards in the pub and they play a major part in bringing in customers.'

The pub games are also an attraction for younger clients. 'There is a group of 16- and 17-year-olds who come in quite regularly,' says Margaret, 'but I tend to turn a blind eye. I know them all, and their parents. I allow them to buy only shandy or beer and if the noise level starts to rise, I will just remind them that I may have to ask them to leave. We understand each other well, and there are seldom any problems.'

*A West German beer hall. The owner of the hall will have much greater control over opening times than a British publican.*

1 Would you say Margaret is being realistic and sensible or foolish and irresponsible in allowing under-age drinkers in her pub?
2 Does the prospect of drinking in a pub appeal to you, and if so, why?
3 Do you think use of the pub is overdone in radio and television 'soap operas'?
4 If pubs are to be used as meeting places, can you think of any ways in which they can be made more acceptable for young people and non-drinkers?

Discuss the following view: 'It is a fact that publicans have more alcohol problems than any other group in Britain, so people should see pubs less as community centres and more as potentially dangerous havens for drug addicts.'

# Drinking and Driving

Drinking considerably increases the chances of having a road accident and particularly of having a serious accident. Detailed investigations of accidents conducted by the Transport and Road Research Laboratory in 1974 showed that one in three drivers killed in accidents had blood alcohol levels above the statutory limit of 80 mg per 100 ml (80 mg%). A more recent estimate suggests that the cost of road accidents involving alcohol amounts to £1,000 million per year. This figure includes damage to vehicles, medical treatment for the injured, sickness benefits, police and court costs and so on. The price in terms of distress and suffering is more difficult to estimate.

In 1967 the Road Traffic Act led to the introduction of the breathalyser. The act states that it is an offence for anyone who has more than 80 mg of alcohol to 100 ml of blood to be in charge of any kind of motor vehicle, whether they be driving it or simply sitting behind the wheel while the car is stationary on the public highway. It is also illegal to 'sleep it off' in a car if the car is parked at a kerb and the person's blood alcohol level is above the limit.

The Road Traffic Act does not allow random breath testing, but the police may stop a car if they have reasonable grounds for suspecting that the driver has been drinking. They may then breathalyse the driver. He or she may be asked to inflate a small polythene bag by blowing through a narrow tube containing special crystals. Should enough of these crystals turn green, the police have the power to arrest the driver who will then be taken to

*A police officer asks a driver suspected of being 'over the limit' to blow into an electronic breathalyser.*

*The police now organize a number of campaigns aimed at educating drivers about the effects of alcohol.*

a police station and tested on a different machine. This is called a substantive machine and its readings are accepted as evidence in court. Only if the driver is very close to the legal limit will a blood test be taken. Another machine, known as an Alcolmeter, is beginning to replace the bag containing crystals in the initial test. This is an electronic device that 'reads' the amount of alcohol in a driver's breath and illuminates a red, green, or amber light, according to the strength of alcohol in the driver's breath.

The police can choose whether or not they press charges against a driver whose blood alcohol level has been found to be too high, but in the vast majority of cases they will do so. The maximum penalty for drinking and driving is now a fine of £1,000 and six months in prison. Someone convicted of this offence is also automatically disqualified from driving.

Although 80 mg% is the legal alcohol limit for driving in Britain, some experts would suggest that this limit is set too high. The risk of having an accident is two times greater for someone with an alcohol level of only 50 mg% than it is for someone who has not been drinking at all. In some Scandinavian countries the legal levels are much lower and the penalties rather tougher than in Britain. This has led to a considerable reduction in the number of people who drink and drive.

Drinking-and-driving offences increase at certain specific times of the year; Christmas and the New Year, for instance, are regarded as being particularly notorious in this connection. As a result, the police have over recent years mounted special campaigns to 'crack down' on the drinking driver. Generally these campaigns are designed around some slogan, the gist of which is: 'If you drive, don't drink.'

# Case Study 4:

# Pauline, aged 18

Pauline has always been the quietest, and the most sensible, of the children in her family. Her two brothers, both older than her, have always been the ones who have been in trouble, both at school and on occasions with the police. That is why she finds it ironic that it is she who has been disqualified from driving.

Pauline describes what happened to her: 'It was just the sort of thing that you hear people laughing about in pubs. The trouble was that I had not expected to pass my driving test first time around; when I did, my first thought was to celebrate. I rang all my friends and we arranged to meet at our local. My brother Ian lent me his car to drive down there.

'I really didn't have much to drink: a couple of beers and then a couple of glasses of wine. I thought I was being careful about how much I drank. Anyway, when closing time came I drove home, taking a couple of friends with me. It was all going well until I came round this sharp corner and suddenly there was another car in my headlights. I swerved, and we ended up in the ditch. Nobody was badly hurt, luckily, but it could have been a lot worse.'

Four months on, Pauline is £200 poorer and will not be allowed to drive again for another year. She had saved some money to buy herself a car, but now she is going to spend it on a holiday. 'The silly thing about all this,' she says, 'is that I don't really like drinking. I drank because I felt I ought to, because everyone else was. I thought people might laugh at me if I didn't.

'My brothers have always drunk far more than I have, and they have never been caught drinking and driving. Ian is always bragging that drink does not affect his driving and he often gives his friends lifts home after spending three or four hours in the pub. My parents are always nagging him to be more careful, but he doesn't take any notice. Yet when I crashed his car, he went mad with me, calling me all sorts of names. He couldn't see that what had happened to me could easily happen to him; he said it was all a matter of individual skill and ability. He will never learn!'

Opposite: *Some pubs have introduced their own breathalysers, so that customers can check if they are fit to drive.*

1 If a person's chances of having an accident are doubled with a blood alcohol level of 50 mg%, do you think the legal limit of 80 mg% is too high?
2 Would you view a drunken driver whose car hit and killed someone as a murderer or as someone who had made a terrible mistake?
3 Do you think sending drinking-and-driving offenders to prison is the best way of dealing with them? If not, what other ways can you suggest?

# Alcohol Dependence

Most people who drink alcohol enjoy doing so and do not experience any problems in connection with their drinking. For a small minority, however, alcohol has become an essential part of life; members of this minority are no longer in control of their drinking, instead the drink is in control of them. These people are dependent on, or addicted to, alcohol.

It is possible to be either physically or psychologically dependent on alcohol, but most people who are physically addicted will be psychologically or emotionally addicted as well. If a person is physically addicted, then he or she has a body that adapts and manages to function even though quite large amounts of alcohol are present in the blood. Dependent drinkers

*A 'typical alcoholic'? In fact, many people who are dependent on alcohol seldom appear to be drunk.*

*One of the most important steps for people who feel their drinking has got out of hand is to seek professional help.*

may be able to control their behaviour so that they appear quite sober, but they have no control over the effects alcohol has on their bodies. They can only function once their alcohol level has been brought up to the level they have become used to. Dependent drinkers also become tolerant to alcohol; this means their bodies require larger and larger doses of alcohol to produce the same effect as they experienced when they first drank. This tolerance for alcohol is rather deceptive. The drinker thinks that as he or she does not get drunk, nothing much can be wrong; in fact, exactly the opposite is true. The body has become dependent on alcohol.

If the alcohol level is not maintained and if the drinker goes without drinking for any length of time, then he or she is likely to suffer withdrawal symptoms. The most common of these are bad nerves, shakiness, sweatiness and nausea. The sufferer may also feel tense, jittery and generally ill. Withdrawal symptoms can be more or less severe depending on the degree of the person's dependence.

It is only in the later stages of dependence that the drinker is likely to experience *delirium tremens* or the D.T.s. The patient suffering from *delirium tremens* will be physically ill, confused and shaking. Seeing visions and hearing voices are also quite common during the 'horrors'.

Psychological dependence occurs when the mind relies upon alcohol for pleasure, happiness and comfort. The feeling that 'I'll be able to cope better once I've had a few drinks' is a symptom of this psychological dependence.

Many of those who have experienced alcohol problems say that it is the psychological rather than the physical dependence that is so hard to deal with. For some people alcohol has become a 'crutch', a way of getting themselves through the day. For others it is so much a part of their social and working lives that avoiding it seems impossible. Learning to say 'no' is not easy.

People who feel that their drinking is beginning to cause problems either for themselves or for their families and friends are best advised to seek help from their general practitioner (G.P.). He or she will know what National Health resources are available in the local area. If the doctor has reason to believe that the patient will suffer from severe withdrawal symptoms, then that patient may be referred to an alcoholism treatment unit. These units are usually attached to hospitals. A variety of drugs may be prescribed to help the patient through the unpleasant withdrawal, or 'drying out', period and there may also be some counselling available to help the patient off his or her psychological dependence on alcohol.

There are also some private alcoholism treatment facilities in Britain. They have programmes which are similar to those available in treatment units run by the National Health Service, but they are fairly expensive. A G.P. can make arrangements for help at one of these units as well.

*Patients at alcoholism units are closely monitored to ensure that they are benefitting from their treatment.*

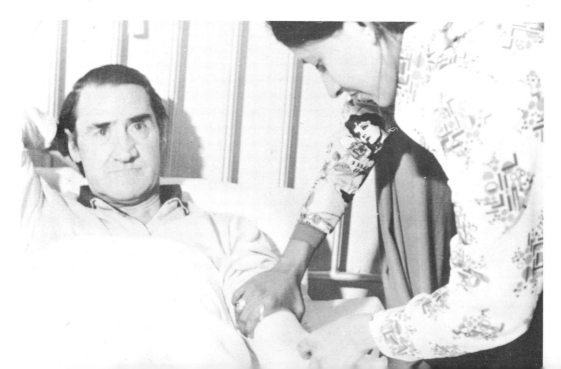

*Group therapy gives those who are dependent on alcohol the chance to talk with others who are experiencing problems similar to their own.*

The best-known agency helping people with alcohol problems is Alcoholics Anonymous (AA). This is a self-help organization in which people with alcohol problems help each other come off drink. Al-Anon, an offshoot of AA, provides support for the families and friends of the drinking person, while Al-Ateen is available for adolescent members of these families.

The National Council on Alcoholism in London and the Scottish Council on Alcoholism in Edinburgh co-ordinate the activities of a network of locally based agencies, which are known as regional councils on alcoholism. These can now be found in most major cities and in some country areas as well. Different regional councils offer different services: some give confidential advice and counselling, while others may just give information and point the caller towards the most suitable treatment facility in their area.

These are the addresses of some of the agencies mentioned in this chapter:

Alcoholics Anonymous, P.O. Box 514, 11 Redcliffe Gardens, London SW10 (Tel: 01-352-9779)

Al-Anon Family Groups (also Al-Ateen), 61 Great Dover Street, London SE1 4YF (Tel: 01-403-0888)

National Council on Alcoholism, 3 Grosvenor Crescent, London SW1X 7EL (Tel: 01-235-4182)

Scottish Council on Alcoholism, 47–49 York Place, Edinburgh EH1 3JD (Tel: 031-556-0459)

Addresses and telephone numbers for local organizations and regional councils can be obtained from the above or from the local telephone directory.

# Case Study 5:

## Mike, aged 30

It is now a year since Mike decided that something had to be done about what he finally came to recognize as his drink problem. It was then that he realized that his drinking was no longer 'social'. 'Unsocial would be more like it,' says Mike. 'I know I was becoming unpleasant to live with, irritable and short-tempered, and I was doing quite a lot of shouting at my wife and kids. But when you are in a situation like that, it is difficult to see objectively quite how far you have gone.'

Mike finds it hard to remember quite how, or why, he started drinking alcohol. When he was in his early teens he would have the odd drink, as much for a dare as anything else, and he was 17 before he suffered his first hangover. 'It was not an experience I enjoyed,' he admits, 'so after that I would just have the occasional pint in the pub with friends, either at lunchtime or in the evening. I always drank beer in those days; I had somehow got the idea that I was alright as long as I stuck to beer. I thought it was spirits that did the damage.'

Mike had married at the age of 25 and he and his wife would usually spend a Friday or Saturday evening in the pub every week. After the birth of their children, however, his wife came out less frequently. At this time Mike also changed his job and it was then that his drinking really increased. 'I was quite often away from home,' he recalls, 'either on my own or entertaining clients. I was usually having my first drink at about 11.30 am.

'It was my wife who commented that I didn't seem to go anywhere without having a drink. To prove to her that I was in control, I stopped drinking when we went on holiday. It gave me quite a fright. After a couple of days I felt shaky, sick and very depressed.'

Mike was eventually persuaded to visit an alcohol counselling agency. He remembers how embarrassed he was when he first attended: 'I kept telling them I wasn't an alcoholic, but eventually I was forced to admit I had a problem. I didn't touch a drop for four months after that. Now I have the occasional drink, but I make decisions about how much I am going to drink before I have the first one; this gives me the feeling that I have some control over alcohol at last.'

Opposite: *The line between regular social drinking and dependence is a fine one.*

1 Do you believe there is such a person as a 'typical alcoholic'? If so, describe one. Justify your description.
2 What do you think parents should do if they think their son or daughter is drinking too much?
3 It is estimated that in Britain about 800,000 to 1,000,000 people have alcohol-related problems. Do you think we should be more concerned than we are about drinking? What do you think we should do about the high number of 'problem drinkers'?

Consider the following argument: 'In some countries breweries are obliged to pay a small percentage of their profits towards financing help for people with alcohol problems. We should adopt this system in Britain. For too long drinks manufacturers have been able to wash their hands of their responsibilities.'

# Choosing to Drink

From the moment we are born there are certain things we need in order to survive. We need to eat, we need to sleep and in Britain, unless we intend living in a very hot room all the year round, we need to wear clothes. In addition to these basic physical requirements, the laws of the land decree that certain things can or cannot be done. The law lays down that we should attend school between the ages of five and sixteen and that we should not steal from or commit acts of violence against other people. If we don't obey the law, actions are taken against us which make life exceedingly unpleasant.

Another aspect of our existence, however, involves choice: we choose to join clubs, to go on holiday, to smoke cigarettes or to drink alcohol. All these things may give us pleasure, but there is no law that insists on our doing them, nor are they essential to our survival. Nevertheless the social pressure to do some of these things, and to drink in particular, is considerable. We are expected to raise our glasses at births, deaths, marriages, birthdays and the crownings of kings and queens; we seal business contracts with a drink; we offer a drink in hospitality when friends visit our homes; and we relax and drink in pubs after a hard day's work. Alcohol is so bound up with our culture and its customs that it seems almost impossible to avoid using it.

*British holiday-makers in a Greek bar. Because drinking is associated with leisure, it is all too easy to confuse our enjoyment of leisure with our feelings about alcohol.*

*The way in which they see adults using alcohol can have a profound effect on children's own ideas about drinking. Do adults therefore have a responsibility to drink sensibly?*

It is important therefore to face the fact that it is our choice to drink. It is also our choice as to where, when, with whom and how we drink. The most important influences on our drinking habits come from our parents. Research evidence shows that children brought up in families where alcohol is not a taboo subject and where parental drinking is controlled and confined to appropriate occasions such as mealtimes are less likely to develop alcohol problems than others. The opposite is seen to be true in children brought up in environments where drinking is either frowned upon or where drunkenness in one or both parents is common.

Perhaps because drinking is so readily connected with social activities, the 'fun' times in our lives, most of us do choose to drink. It is only somewhere in the vicinity of 10 per cent of the British population that is teetotal. Of this 10 per cent, some will not drink because alcohol does not agree with them, some will make the choice for moral reasons and others because they simply do not like the taste.

So that our drinking years will be enjoyable ones both for ourselves and for our families and friends, it is essential that we teach ourselves or are taught sensible drinking practices. When we learn to drive, we are taught driving skills that allow us to drive safely, so that we endanger neither ourselves nor other people. It is perhaps useful to look at learning to drink in much the same light. The guidelines that follow could be useful in this respect.

It is wise to drink only in moderation and to set the limits of your drinking before taking the first drink. After two or three drinks it will be too late for this, as the alcohol will have begun to influence the decision. It is also sensible to eat a good meal, preferably before you drink but if not then while you are drinking. This slows down the rate of absorption of the alcohol into the blood stream.

Drink slowly. If you are the sort of person who likes to have a glass in your hand, then have something non-alcoholic in between the alcoholic drinks. Alternatively, top up beer or lager with lemonade—it will look much the same colour. Remember that different drinks have different percentages of alcohol in them. Contrary to popular belief, mixing drinks does not make you more drunk—alcohol is alcohol—but it does make it more difficult to keep track of exactly how much you have consumed. It is always better to stick to a drink you know. If you socialize with different groups of people, then watch how much you are drinking. You may find that you speed up your drinking when you are with certain people.

If you are the host or hostess always offer a choice of drinks, non-alcoholic as well as alcoholic. This makes it easier for the guest who for various reasons prefers not to drink alcohol. Remember that some people find it very hard to say 'no'.

*This woman, after drinking five 'shorts', is no longer capable of making decisions about how much she should drink.*

If you are intending to drive then do not drink. Share the driving with friends, so that you can take it in turns to drink. That way everybody gets to enjoy themselves and nobody gets killed.

*By following common-sense rules when it comes to drinking, we can derive a good deal of pleasure and enjoyment from a substance which, when misused, can cause misery and suffering.*

1 Do you think most people drink alcohol because they want to or because they are expected to?
2 If you were at a party and a friend refused an alcoholic drink, how would you view your friend?
3 Do you think that after reading this book, you will be able to make certain decisions about alcohol and how you are going to use it? What will they be?

# Glossary

**Addiction** The inability to cope without a drug such as alcohol.

**Ale** A kind of beer that does not contain hops.

**Beneficial** Having a good result.

**Blood alcohol level** The amount of alcohol in a person's blood, measured in mg per 100 ml of blood. The legal limit for someone driving a car is 80 mg per 100 ml (80 mg%).

**Breathalyser** A bag into which people breathe in order to determine the amount of alcohol in their breath.

**Delirium tremens** The condition experienced by excessive drinkers when they severely limit or stop their drinking. The sufferer may become physically ill, agitated, confused and may see visions and hear voices.

**Dependence** Another word for addiction. Alcoholics are often described as being alcohol-dependent.

**Distillation** The process by which a fermented liquid is heated so that alcohol is given off as a vapour which is then cooled and recollected. This distilled alcohol forms the base of spirits.

**Fermentation** The process by which alcohol is produced. Yeast fungi ferment certain sugars contained in fruits and produce carbon dioxide and alcohol.

**Hops** The dried flowers of the hop plant which are used to give some beers their characteristic bitter flavour.

**Licensed premises** Pubs, clubs etc. which have a licence to sell alcohol that can be drunk there and then. Certain supermarkets and shops (off-licences) may have licences to sell drink for consumption off their premises.

**Licensing laws** The laws which state where and when alcoholic drinks may be sold.

**Measure** One-twenty-fourth of a pint.

**Percentage by volume** The system by which the percentage of alcohol in a drink is measured.

**Perry** A drink made from pears which is similar in taste to cider.

**Publican** The landlord or landlady who either owns or is in charge of a pub.

**Statutory** Laid down by law.

**Teetotal** Never drinking alcohol.

**Tolerance** The body's ability to become used to growing amounts of substances such as alcohol.

**Volatile** Having a low boiling point and thus easily becoming a vapour.

**Withdrawal symptoms** Unpleasant symptoms which occur after someone who is alcohol-dependent stops drinking. The symptoms can vary considerably and may last for a few hours or for several days.

**Yeast** A fungus used in fermentation.

# Further Reading

**Non-fiction:**

*Addiction in the News* by Vanora Leigh (Wayland, 1983)

*Alcohol and Alcoholism—the Report of a Special Committee of the Royal College of Psychiatrists* (Tavistock Publications, 1979)

*Problem Drinking—the New Approach* by Nick Heather and Ian Robertson (Pelican, 1985)

*The Use of Drugs* by Brian Ward (Macdonald, 1086)

*Women and Alcohol* by the Camberwell Council on Alcoholism (Tavistock Publications, 1980)

*Your Everyday Drugs* by W. Bracken (BBC Publications, 1978)

**Fiction:**

*Bogie* by Joe Hyams (Mayflower, 1973)

*Days of Wine and Roses* by D. Westheimer (Corgi, 1963)

*Down and Out in Paris and London* by George Orwell (Penguin, 1969)

*The Magician* by G. Simenon (translated by H. Sebba) (Hamish Hamilton, 1974)

# Acknowledgements

The publishers would like to thank the following for providing the illustrations in this book: Barnaby's Picture Library 7, 15, 19, 21, 36, 41; Camera Talks (Oxford) Ltd 27, 37, 38, 39, 43, 44; J. Allan Cash 5, 6, 28, 29; Mary Evans Picture Library 9, 10, 11, 26; Tim Humphrey *front cover*; Metropolitan Police 32; Topham 4, 12, 22, 23, 25, 33, 35; Malcolm S. Walker 8, 14, 17; Wayland Picture Library 16, 31; Zefa 13, 20, 42, 45.

# Index